Ease Your Life
The Ultimate Guide to Choosing Ease

Najja Ogunshola

Contents

You Deserve a Life of Ease

YOU DESERVE A LIFE of ease. You deserve the kind of life where you radiate joy, where you feel in control, and have peace with your purpose and destiny on this earth.

And yet, in this day and age, we are used to living anything *but*. We live our lives surrounded by stress, inundated by deadlines, people expecting things from us, and constant demands from life. We live in ways that leave us feeling overwhelmed almost all the time, and yet, we don't always know what we can do to feel better about ourselves. This is why we often need more introspection. We live our day-to-day lives too quickly, and we rarely take the time to just *stop*, look around, and figure things out. If you completely relate to this, I have great news for you: you have come to the right place.

Stress kills. You might feel like this is completely over-the-top as a statement, but it's true – stress is a silent killer. Why? Because it brings along several symptoms and potential consequences that affect our health in many ways. For example, chronic stress –stress that you constantly feel – can lead to high levels of inflammation, which increase your chances of developing health problems such as heart disease, stroke, obesity, diabetes, and high blood pressure.[1]

Despite that, stress is something we do not pay *nearly* enough attention to. And why is that? Why do we underplay the role that stress plays on our health? Well, this is in part because we live in a day and age where stress is just *accepted*. It's "normal" to be stressed because of our work. It's normal to be stressed because we are working too much, have too many deadlines, or are being asked to do things that are completely outside our capacity by our boss. It's normal to be stressed because we barely have the time to cook dinner, so we end up getting food from the local restaurant near our home and feel *worse* because we eat food that isn't great for us. All these things are considered normal...when in reality, they aren't – they are clearly showing us that something's wrong. If you don't have time to eat, to sleep properly, to take care of yourself, it's expected that you'll feel poorly about yourself.

1. https://www.mayoclinic.org/healthy-lifestyle/stress-management/in-depth/stress-symptoms/art-20050987#:~:text=Common%20effects%20of%20stress,%2C%20stroke%2C%20obesity%20and%20diabetes.

But this is where self-care comes in! You deserve to live a life in which you feel calm, serene, and *at ease*. Nevertheless, it's not as easy as it sounds. Otherwise, we would *all* be living such a life.

So, where do we start? How can you get a life in which you feel more at ease? This is what this book is here to help you achieve. The goal of this book is to help you question the things in your life that are making you live the way you do. For example, do you lack the time to self-care because you prioritize work and money too much, or at the expense of your health? Do you live every day extremely stressed because you don't make the time to relax? Why do you feel this way? These are the kinds of questions that you will be invited to ask yourself throughout the next few pages.

But this book is unlike others. It's about more than just questioning yourself introspectively – it is rooted in the art of *shadow work*. As such, throughout the next few sections, we will be applying notions of shadow work to your journey of ease.

Throughout the next few sections, we will be looking at a few facets involved in this journey of reaching a life of ease. First, we will explore the discovery stage, where you discover your inner world, including your shadows, desires, and ease. Second, we will jump into the transformation, where you will be prompted with a few questions to integrate your shadows and transform your life towards ease. In the harmony section, we will uncover strategies and practices to cultivate inner peace, balance, and harmonious living. Then, in the reflection section, we will start reflecting on your journey, insights, and the transformations you are experiencing in pursuit of ease. In the next section, we will look at empowerment, namely at confidence, resilience, and renewal of mindset. Finally, in the sixth section, we will work on mindfulness and alignment, so you can align your values, actions, and life situations with your journey towards ease.

The idea is to help you spend more time self-caring, and using this journal to reflect is a great way to do so. Take some time by yourself and show yourself that you care enough about your own well-being to prioritize self-discovery.

Are you ready for more ease?

If so, it's time to turn the page...

Discovery

TO FIX SOMETHING, WE first need to know what's broken. This is exactly why the first section of this workbook is all about discovery – discovering what your inner world is like, including your shadows and your desires. But before we jump into this section, let's explore what *shadow work* is in more depth.

Shadow work is a self-help process. It was introduced by Carl Jung, a Swiss psychiatrist. It is about exploring and integrating the shadow aspect of your psyche – the *suppressed, denied, or unseen* parts of yourself. The shadow holds our repressed emotions, desires, and our traits, all things that we may have learned to hide or to deny, be it because of what we think society, or our family expects from us, or because of what *we* expect from ourselves. So, when we do shadow work, we try to uncover these parts of ourselves, and we try to understand them. We therefore develop who we are holistically – i.e., in the bigger picture, or as a whole – and work towards healing ourselves.

In this workbook, we are using shadow work to help you move towards a life of ease. You are going to be prompted to confront and integrate the unacknowledged aspects of yourself. That might include addressing your internal conflicts, traumas, or any suppressed emotions that you might have which could be acting as barriers to experiencing ease or fulfillment with your life.

So, take each prompt as they come to you. Allow yourself to fully be immersed in them. Allow yourself to discover who you *truly* are. Don't fall back into what you think society wants from you, or what you *think* you deserve. Focus on what *you* want. This process should allow you to accept yourself, to *understand* yourself, and to embrace *all* facets of your being. Integrating the shadow self can help you develop more emotional intelligence, resilience, and makes you a more authentic person because you learn to better *know* yourself.

Self-Affirmation

I move through my journey of discovery with ease and openness, welcoming new understandings about myself and the world.

Reflect on aspects of yourself that you keep hidden from others.

Unfortunately, many of us tend to hide parts of ourselves from others, whether it's because we are worried about their reaction, what they might tell us, or how they might think of us after they find out about these aspects of our personality. Why do you feel the need to hide these parts of yourself? Think about how acknowledging them might bring more ease in your interactions. Think about how great it would be to be fully yourself, without worrying about having to hide parts of yourself!

_____

_____

_____

_____

_____

_____

_____

_____

_____

_____

_____

_____

_____

_____

_____

Take some time to think about your deepest desires, the ones that you have never expressed.

How do you feel about them, and how might bringing them to light create a more genuine life experience? What if, instead of pushing them down and thinking of them as unachievable, you switched your mindset and just focused on what you *can* achieve? It's all about the mindset!

_____

_____

_____

_____

_____

_____

_____

_____

_____

_____

_____

_____

_____

_____

Think about the dreams you had as a child but gave up as you grew up.

How do these forgotten dreams resonate with your current self, and can revisiting them bring more happiness into your life? Are you currently doing something that is considered "good" by society, but that doesn't really align with the dreams you used to have and *still* have deep down inside?

_____

_____

_____

_____

_____

_____

_____

_____

_____

_____

_____

_____

_____

_____

Have a look at the fears that are hidden in your subconscious.

How have these fears influenced the decisions you've made throughout
your life? How might addressing them create a path that is more
conducive to living in ease?

_____

_____

_____

_____

_____

_____

_____

_____

_____

_____

_____

_____

_____

_____

Explore the emotions you often hide from others, or the emotions you try to avoid having by suppressing them.

How do these emotions impact your well-being, and how might *acknowledging* them open doors to more emotional connectivity? Do you think you could spend more time journaling? (Using this journal is a great step!)

_____

_____

_____

_____

_____

_____

_____

_____

_____

_____

_____

_____

_____

_____

Reflect on the memories you've buried deep within.

How do these memories continue to influence your present, and can bringing them back up help you heal from old wounds, traumas, or bad experiences? For example, think about how old experiences in school – which is often a foundational experience that affects many of us for the rest of our lives – might have affected who you are today. Or perhaps you had a bad relationship that still affects who you are to this day. Be honest with yourself, and allow yourself to revisit these memories, if they help you uncover hidden parts of yourself.

_____

_____

_____

_____

_____

_____

_____

_____

_____

_____

_____

_____

_____

_____

Contemplate the pains you've kept hidden away.

How has concealing this pain affected your journey, and how might addressing it help you develop more resilience? Look, we're all human. We *all* hide some of the pain we feel because it's often much easier than confronting it head-on. But these pains are there for a reason – they remind us that we have emotions and that we are affected by them. So, think about these pains and allow yourself to fully feel them. Do you feel like a weight has been lifted off your shoulders?

_____

_____

_____

_____

_____

_____

_____

_____

_____

_____

_____

_____

_____

Take a moment to think about the secret aspirations that you hesitate to go for.

How do these align with your true self, and can embracing them lead to a life of more ease? If you spend your entire life wishing you were doing something else, or wishing you were *someone* else, you aren't living a life that is truly authentic and truly representative of who you are. Life's too short to live only half of what you want to live because you're scared of trying something different, or of going against the status quo. Why are you hesitating? What's stopping you?

_____

_____

_____

_____

_____

_____

_____

_____

_____

_____

_____

_____

_____

_____

_____

Focus on the strengths you have that you've neglected to appreciate.

How can recognizing these help make you more confident and help you in the various facets of your life? Which strengths do you think you may have been ignoring? Do you think you ignore them because you don't believe in them? These strengths can help bring more ease into your life, so make sure to know what they are!

_____

_____

_____

_____

_____

_____

_____

_____

_____

_____

_____

_____

_____

_____

Consider the weaknesses you try to hide.

We've talked about your strengths, but now, it's time to think about the weaknesses you have. How might *embracing* these flaws lead to personal growth and a more balanced life? Can you work on accepting these flaws? Can you work towards appreciating these flaws and not blaming yourself for having them in the first place? These are a *part* of you—they aren't necessarily something to be fixed.

_____

_____

_____

_____

_____

_____

_____

_____

_____

_____

_____

_____

_____

_____

_____

Think about the invisible chains that restrict you.

How have they shaped who you are, who you have become over the past few years, and how might they also affect who you will become in the future? Do you think that breaking free from them could make you feel freer? Chains might be, for example, negative self-talk, low confidence, imposter syndrome... The list goes on.

_____

_____

_____

_____

_____

_____

_____

_____

_____

_____

_____

_____

_____

_____

Think about the opinions and thoughts you silence.

How might giving voice to these thoughts help you more authentically
be yourself? We all have things we hide. We all have opinions that we keep
to ourselves out of fear of being judged. But what if voicing them is the
solution? What if by voicing these opinions, you end up surrounded by
people who share your opinions, instead of being surrounded by people
whose opinions you feel wouldn't match yours?

_____

_____

_____

_____

_____

_____

_____

_____

_____

_____

_____

_____

_____

_____

Think about the things you really love but might be avoiding because you feel guilty, or you are worried about what other people would say.

How might allowing yourself these things bring more joy and satisfaction into your life? We often worry way too much about what other people think, want, or what they might say about what we do. And yet, in reality, we're often *way* too focused on ourselves to think about what other people might be doing, so they're probably not thinking about you either. So, do what you love.

_____

_____

_____

_____

_____

_____

_____

_____

_____

_____

_____

_____

Think about the talents you may have that you still haven't figured out.

How can discovering these enrich your life and bring you a sense of accomplishment? We all have talents that we haven't found yet. However, you might have a few guiding points. For example, if people have given you compliments on certain things, think about whether that might be a hidden talent. The more you discover these things about yourself, the more you can also explore them further and bring more ease into your life. Why? Because the more you fill your life with things you are *good* at and things you enjoy, the more you feel fulfilled. Life should be enjoyed!

_____

_____

_____

_____

_____

_____

_____

_____

_____

_____

_____

Consider the passions you've neglected over time.

Do you think you would benefit from bringing them back into your life? For example, if you used to love going ice skating, if you were a great dancer, or if you used to love going for runs but stopped because you didn't have enough time, now's the time to think about how to reintroduce it into your life. This is *also* part of your self-care. You bring ease into your life when you realize that doing things that you love and enjoy doing is just as important as working, making money, or looking for success.

_____

_____

_____

_____

_____

_____

_____

_____

_____

_____

_____

_____

_____

Transformation

WELCOME TO THE SECOND section of this workbook. So far, you have explored and discovered more about yourself. You have started to better understand why you do certain things, why you think a certain way, and why you might avoid saying or doing things. This is all important as part of shadow work.

Now that you have *discovered* yourself to a greater extent, it's time to *transform* yourself further into someone better. Note that I didn't say someone *new* – you are great the way you are, and you do not need to completely reinvent yourself. However, you *can* benefit from transforming parts of your life that you are not entirely happy about, so as to feel better about your life and thus *yourself*.

We are not transforming you entirely. We are transforming the parts of yourself that you aren't happy about, such as the way you might hold back from doing something because of negative beliefs about yourself, or how you may avoid taking opportunities out of fear of failure or of looking like an imposter. We are transforming these parts of you and your life to make you and your life something even greater!

Self-Affirmation

I cultivate positivity and joy, creating a life of ease and abundance.

Reflect on a viewpoint you held that has gone through a transformation.

How has this change in perspective influenced your decisions and relationships, and how can remaining open to change contribute to your ongoing betterment? In other words, have you ever had a perspective that changed, and if so, why? Do you think it was a good change? Do you think this is a transformation that you could benefit from in other aspects of your life? How can you make this happen?

_____

_____

_____

_____

_____

_____

_____

_____

_____

_____

_____

_____

Think of a vulnerability you have recently realized you have.

Have you learned how to embrace it? If so, how has embracing it affected your sense of self and interactions with others? Do you feel more at ease knowing that you have a vulnerability, but that it is nothing that you necessarily *need* to change? Accepting that you have vulnerabilities is a great way to control how they make you feel. Think of using positive affirmations to reinforce this feeling of acceptance so you are less affected by them and more in control of the effect they have on your mood or sense of self.

_____

_____

_____

_____

_____

_____

_____

_____

_____

_____

_____

_____

Think about a failure you've experienced.

How can you *reframe* this failure as a learning opportunity, and how can this transformation in perspective promote resilience and growth? For example, if you recently had a bad experience with a job, or if you lost a client, how can you reframe this so you can *learn* from the experience? Transform these experiences into learning opportunities.

Reflect on a limiting belief you have transformed into an empowering one.

Limiting beliefs are the ones we have that make us doubt ourselves, or that make us speak negatively of ourselves. How has this shift influenced your actions and outlook on life? How can you use this and apply it to other limiting beliefs? Think about the prompts you responded to in the "Discovery" section, such as the ones regarding your dreams or aspirations and why you aren't seeing them through.

_____

_____

_____

_____

_____

_____

_____

_____

_____

_____

_____

_____

_____

Think about a part of yourself you have recently accepted, even if in the past, you disliked it and did everything in your power to avoid it.

How has accepting this part transformed your self-image? Has it made you feel more at peace with yourself? Has it made you feel more at ease? For example, let's say that you recently came to terms with your body image and finally decided to stop worrying about your weight. How did this feel? How has it changed how you view yourself? Can you apply this to other parts of your life?

_____

_____

_____

_____

_____

_____

_____

_____

_____

_____

_____

_____

_____

_____

_____

Consider a wound you have started to heal.

It might be a part of trauma that you experienced in your life, or a bad experience, such as bullying, that you are now healing. How has the process of healing transformed your emotional reaction to similar triggers, and how can this experience help you feel more prepared for the future? Can you apply the lessons you've learned to other aspects of your life?

_____

_____

_____

_____

_____

_____

_____

_____

_____

_____

_____

_____

_____

Think of a situation where being mindful led to a better outcome.

Mindfulness is something we will dive into more deeply in the upcoming sections. For now, consider situations where you focused on the *present* moment instead of focusing on the past or the future. Maybe you were anxious, or maybe you felt overwhelmed, and you used mindfulness to bring you back to the present. Can you apply this to other situations you are experiencing and transform them into better ones?

_____

_____

_____

_____

_____

_____

_____

_____

_____

_____

_____

_____

_____

Reflect on a desire that has evolved over time.

Reaching success, becoming rich, getting your revenge on the people who treated you poorly in high school... Now, you're seeing it all completely differently. You've risen above, and you no longer care enough to get revenge. You appreciate success, but it's not what dictates your life. How has this transformation affected your pursuit of happiness and alignment with your true self?

Think about a strength you have recently worked on and gotten even better at.

How has improving his strength transformed your approach to challenges and contributed to achieving your goals with more ease? Do you think you could do this with other strengths? Which ones?

_____

_____

_____

_____

_____

_____

_____

_____

_____

_____

_____

_____

_____

_____

Think of a moment when you started feeling a lot more compassionate about something or someone.

Did you feel more at ease? We live in a world that's highly focused on success and being "better" than other people. Unfortunately, that also means that we can end up being totally focused on ourselves. In fact, you might have caught yourself congratulating your friends for their accomplishments while silently thinking about how jealous you were. Now, if you've transformed into a more empathetic person, how does it feel? If you haven't yet, what can you do to reach that point? Trust me, life feels far better when you truly feel empathetic towards people!

_____

_____

_____

_____

_____

_____

_____

_____

_____

_____

_____

_____

Consider a step you've taken towards loving yourself more.

How has nurturing self-love affected your self-worth and interactions with the world? Are you kinder to others? Kinder to yourself? How was that experience, and how can you apply these learnings to other aspects of your life?

_____

_____

_____

_____

_____

_____

_____

_____

_____

_____

_____

_____

_____

_____

_____

Reflect on how your sense of purpose has become clearer.

Do you feel like you are more aware of your purpose? Do you feel like you know yourself better? How has this clarification in purpose guided your life decisions and provided direction in your journey? If it hasn't, what do you think you need to transform that aspect of your life?

_____

_____

_____

_____

_____

_____

_____

_____

_____

_____

_____

_____

_____

_____

_____

Think of a change you've made to improve your health.

How has prioritizing your physical well-being transformed your energy levels and overall life satisfaction? Do you feel better about yourself and in your body when you treat it well? When you exercise? Or perhaps you quit vaping, smoking, drinking, and so on?

_____

_____

_____

_____

_____

_____

_____

_____

_____

_____

_____

_____

_____

_____

Reflect on an experience that has built your resilience.

How has becoming more resilient transformed your approach to challenges? Has it helped you feel better about yourself? Do you feel like you can take on any challenge?

_____

_____

_____

_____

_____

_____

_____

_____

_____

_____

_____

_____

_____

_____

_____

Harmony

TO LIVE A LIFE at ease, you need to find *harmony*. In other words, you need to find *balance*, and this balance can be hard to achieve. We're living days where we jump from one place to another non-stop. We drive hastily to work while we drop coffee on our shirts, and we run to the nearby restaurant to grab a quick lunch that we will eat while remaining glued to our laptops over our "break." These habits aren't synonymous with a life that's balanced. So, we need to take a good look at what we need to change to bring more balance to our lives. This includes, among others, the following:

-Time to take care of yourself *physically*. Yes, you're busy. But no matter how busy you are, your physical health should still remain a top priority. Why? Because without physical health, you have nothing. You can't go to work, you can't take care of yourself, you can't go grocery shopping, and you might even need to rely on other people to take care of you. You're not invincible!

-Time to take care of yourself *mentally*. Yes, your mental health is important. The same way you wouldn't expect yourself to walk on a broken leg, you can't function as well if your brain isn't functioning the right way. If your mental health is down the drain, it's time to get some help.

... time to relax. That means *self-care*. Life is not always about working. You work to live—you don't live to work. You need some time to just chill sometimes. Maybe that's by yourself, or maybe it's with other people – whatever's best for you!

... time to take care of your responsibilities. This is also a form of self-care. Self-care is not always about taking a bubble bath and putting on a moisturizing face mask. Sometimes, it really is as simple as taking a day to do your laundry, meal prep, and work on the tasks that you've been procrastinating for a month.

As you respond to the next few prompts, be mindful of what *you* do to stay balanced.

Self-Affirmation

I accept all of life's experiences with grace and ease, learning and growing with every step I take.

Reflect on how you've balanced your energies recently.

Do you feel like this internal balance has harmonized your external world? Do you think this balance is influencing your interactions and experiences? Do you feel more at peace?

_____

_____

_____

_____

_____

_____

_____

_____

_____

_____

_____

_____

Consider a time you felt in sync with life's rhythm.

You know what these moments feel like. Everything seems to just be working perfectly. Work is going well, your relationship is doing great, and overall, you're having a *really good time.* What do you think brought this on? Do you feel like you could return to this?

_____

_____

_____

_____

_____

_____

_____

_____

_____

_____

_____

_____

Explore a time when you were actively working on your inner peace.

How has fostering this tranquility within yourself harmonized your *outer* world? Did it often result in more serene and meaningful experiences? Did you feel like you were at peace with others because you felt at peace *inside* first and foremost?

_____

_____

_____

_____

_____

_____

_____

_____

_____

_____

_____

_____

_____

_____

_____

Look at how you've created synergy in your relationships.

How has building mutually-enhancing connections fostered deeper understanding and harmony in your interactions?

_____

_____

_____

_____

_____

_____

_____

_____

_____

_____

_____

_____

_____

_____

Think about a situation where your intentions and actions were in perfect harmony.

How did this alignment influence the outcome and your overall satisfaction and peace? Specifically, did you feel like because you were aligned, everything worked out well? If so, why do you think that was the case?

_____

_____

_____

_____

_____

_____

_____

_____

_____

_____

_____

_____

_____

_____

Think of the steps you've taken to harmonize your environment.

How has that influenced your mood, productivity, and overall well-being? When we make sure that everything is well-balanced, we also feel a *lot* more anchored. These steps might be cleaning your environment, cooking more often, hiring someone to help you with the cleaning, and so on. Do what you've got to do!

_____

_____

_____

_____

_____

_____

_____

_____

_____

_____

_____

_____

_____

_____

_____

Reflect on your values and how you live them daily.

Do you feel like aligning your actions with your core beliefs helps you stay more balanced? Do you feel like you are out of balance when you don't act in a way that aligns with your values? How can you address this? Can you change this at all?

_____

_____

_____

_____

_____

_____

_____

_____

_____

_____

_____

_____

_____

Think about how maintaining emotional balance has impacted your life – or could impact your life.

If you've been especially good at calming your emotions and staying grounded, congratulate yourself! How does it feel? Do you feel like it is helping you stay balanced in other aspects of your life?

_____

_____

_____

_____

_____

_____

_____

_____

_____

_____

_____

_____

_____

_____

Reflection

Throughout this workbook, you have been continuously asked to reflect on what you think, who you are, who you want to be, and the like. These are all forms of reflection. Now, however, you will be asked to reflect on your life thus far, as well as the changes you've experienced so far having gone through this book.

Reflection is crucial for your personal development. It is how you can pinpoint what you have worked on, and where you could improve. Likewise, it *also* shows you what you've done well so far; hence, what to congratulate yourself on.

Self-Affirmation

I attract abundance and prosperity with ease, and my life is filled with endless opportunities.

Reflect on how your life experiences mirror your inner world.

How have your thoughts, emotions, and beliefs been mirrored back to you through your interactions and experiences? Do you think this has made you more self-aware? For example, do you often find yourself surrounded by people whose values and mindsets don't align with yours? If so, how did this present itself?

Often, life mirrors who we are, how we react, and what we think. It gives us more negativity if we keep being negative. It makes us sadder if we are constantly sad and don't actively work on being happy. Pay attention to what you are putting out into the world.

_____

_____

_____

_____

_____

_____

_____

_____

_____

_____

_____

_____

How have your experiences shaped your development, and what reflections have been crucial in understanding yourself better?

We all grow through life. We (hopefully!) become better people as time goes by. Throughout this process, many things affect who we are as people. The experiences we have change how we think, and hence, who we are. What have you experienced that has changed you deeply?

_____

_____

_____

_____

_____

_____

_____

_____

_____

_____

_____

_____

_____

_____

Reflect on the significant changes you have undergone.

Now, let's go a bit deeper. How have these transformations impacted your perspectives, values, and overall sense of self? What insights have they provided? As mentioned in the previous prompt, we all go through experiences that completely change us. We go through things that make us more resilient. But these can also change your values and how you see the world!

_____

_____

_____

_____

_____

_____

_____

_____

_____

_____

_____

_____

_____

Explore the ways in which you have come to understand yourself better.

How has this deeper reflection enriched your life? Has it given you more self-acceptance and self-love? Do you now feel more at ease, knowing that you fully know yourself and appreciate yourself the way you are?

_____

_____

_____

_____

_____

_____

_____

_____

_____

_____

_____

_____

_____

_____

Think about the reflections your relationships have given you about your needs, desires, and boundaries.

How have these given you healthier, more fulfilling connections? Do you pay attention to the people you surround yourself with now? Do you pay attention to the kinds of friends you have? Have you left out the people who do not make you feel good about yourself?

Look back on your life decisions and their outcomes. How have your reflections on these decisions provided clarity, learning, and a better understanding of your life path?

The decisions we make are always grounded in some kind of thinking. Even when we're impulsive, we're planning: we choose to do this because it's what we *want* to do, even if it's not the best choice we could be making. Do you feel like you have a clearer view of your life once you reflect on those decisions?

_____

_____

_____

_____

_____

_____

_____

_____

_____

_____

_____

_____

_____

_____

_____

_____

Reflect on past experiences with a fresh perspective, such as by looking back at your responses to previous prompts.

How has revisiting and re-evaluating past events contributed to healing? Do you feel like you understand yourself better?

_____

_____

_____

_____

_____

_____

_____

_____

_____

_____

_____

_____

_____

_____

_____

Consider the times you've been especially resilient.

Do you feel like the reflections on your resilience made you grow as a person? Do you feel empowered? What could you have done better? What may have hindered that resilience?

_____

_____

_____

_____

_____

_____

_____

_____

_____

_____

_____

_____

_____

_____

_____

Think of the mistakes you've made, and the lessons learned.

How have your reflections on these mistakes given you insights? Do you try to think about these mistakes to figure out what you can learn from them? If not, perhaps now is the time to think more about how you can reflect on them!

Empowerment

IMAGINE A LIFE IN which you feel constantly empowered and proud of yourself. This is a life where you feel deeply sure of yourself, in all kinds of situations. You are proud of who you are, what you do, and you feel secure in your way of *being*. You walk with your head held high, and you walk down the street proudly, knowing that you are secure in who you are, what you stand for, and what you believe in. You are *empowered* because you feel powerful.

You don't let things like negative self-talk or limiting beliefs hold you back. These expressions aren't even part of your vocabulary. You stand by what you say, and when people challenge you, you feel like you can support your arguments and opinions without backing down. You speak loudly, and *proudly*, and you don't allow people to tone-police you, or make you feel like you don't have a place where you are. You are *empowered*, because you don't let people stop you from doing what you want, saying what you say, and believing what you believe.

You support other people too, because you know that confident and empowered people don't feel threatened by others. Collaboration leads to better ideas, and teamwork leads to great outcomes. You support other people who are now where you once were because you wish someone had done the same for you, too. You are *empowered* because you don't shy away from empowering others.

Self-Affirmation

I effortlessly step into my power, embracing ease as I confidently manifest my highest potential and purpose.

Think about a moment when you felt your inner power spark up within you!

How did this empowerment make you act differently—*perceive* things differently? How can you channel this power to overcome future tough times and challenges?

_____

_____

_____

_____

_____

_____

_____

_____

_____

_____

_____

_____

_____

_____

_____

Explore the ways you have used your inherent strengths for different means.

How has using your strengths – your great time management skills, your excellent communication – empowered you to achieve your goals and navigate life with confidence and resilience? We all have all kinds of strengths, but the extent to which you know how to use these to your advantage is incredibly important! If you haven't done so yet, start thinking about how you can use your strengths better.

_____

_____

_____

_____

_____

_____

_____

_____

_____

_____

_____

_____

Think about the steps you've taken to build trust in yourself.

It's difficult to trust yourself, especially if you aren't used to believing in yourself through and through! Think about what you've done so far to trust yourself more. Would you say that you tend to trust yourself more than anything? Do you feel like you struggle to trust yourself? For example, do you often feel like an imposter at work, or do you feel like you belong, whatever situation you might be in?

_____

_____

_____

_____

_____

_____

_____

_____

_____

_____

_____

_____

Think of a time you claimed your space assertively.

How did embracing your right to express your thoughts, needs, and desires empower you? Did you feel like you had the space to create healthier, more equitable relationships? Did you feel like you belonged in that environment? We all struggle once in a while to take the space we deserve to take. After all, most of us are used to making ourselves smaller—especially women! And yet, you need to claim your space. So, think about it. When did you last claim your space? When did you *not* claim it, and why? What held you back from doing so?

_____

_____

_____

_____

_____

_____

_____

_____

_____

_____

_____

_____

_____

Look at how you define your worth independent of external opinions.

Yes, this one's hard! It's only in our human nature to focus on our worth based on what other people agree it is. But think *beyond* that for a bit. How do you see your value? How do you value yourself, and how do you make sure that you feel valuable even if someone tries to make you feel less-than?

_____

_____

_____

_____

_____

_____

_____

_____

_____

_____

_____

_____

_____

_____

_____

_____

Think of all the limiting beliefs you have overcome.

What were they, and how did you achieve this? What did you do differently this time? How does it make you feel? What can you learn from this experience so you can apply it to other, similar limiting beliefs?

_____

_____

_____

_____

_____

_____

_____

_____

_____

_____

_____

_____

_____

_____

_____

_____

_____

Think about a time when you empowered others.

The more you are ready to empower others, the more you get to feel empowered yourself! Trust me, there's something incredibly empowering about helping others get to the places *they* want to get to. So, think of how you may have empowered someone else. How did it feel to realize that people were looking up to you and that you could help someone else?

_____

_____

_____

_____

_____

_____

_____

_____

_____

_____

***Reflect on whether you've grown more self-reliant over the past few weeks and months.**￼*

Do you feel like you have become better at relying on yourself, and at trusting that you can do whatever you wish to achieve? On the other hand, if you have always been very self-reliant, do you feel like you could benefit from becoming better at relying on *other people* instead of doing everything on your own? What can you actively do to address this?

Mindfulness and Alignment

FINALLY, WE COME TO the last section of this workbook. Here, we are focusing on being in the present moment and aligning your actions with your values. We are working towards uncovering the beliefs you have that may be holding you back from being fully present in the moment, and from being fully *yourself*. We are ensuring that you are not putting parts of yourself aside only to make other people happy. You are mindful of who you are, how you act, and the situations that tend to affect you or the way you act.

If you change your opinion when you're with certain people just to avoid fights and disagreements, you become mindful of this and change this habit. If you tend to live entirely focused on the future and forget to appreciate what's happening *right now*, you learn to change this and to become more anchored. You learn to appreciate the small joys you are experiencing *today*.

You observe your thoughts without judgment. You meditate when you feel that you need grounding. You give yourself space, and you treat yourself with kindness. Mindfulness is about exactly this. It's about learning to bring your attention to the *present moment*. You want to be open, curious, and avoid judgment. You are entirely aware of the *now*, of your thoughts, feelings, and the sensations you are feeling. You can do this through meditation practices, or as you journal in the next few pages.

Self-Affirmation

I live authentically and true to myself, making my journey through life seamless and filled with ease.

Reflect on a moment when being present transformed your experience entirely.

How did this mindfulness impact your understanding and response to the situation? For example, you might have been extremely stressed about something that happened to you, and instead of being anxious, you decided to be mindful and to bring your mind back to the present. You decided to focus on the *here* and *now*, instead of fixating on whatever happened. How did this change your experience?

_____

_____

_____

_____

_____

_____

_____

_____

_____

_____

_____

_____

Consider a situation where aligning your actions with your values had a significant impact.

Let's consider alignment for a second. How did this *alignment* influence the outcome? Do you feel like the outcome was better because you acted in line with your values? For example, did you have to remove friends because they did something that was out of line? How did it feel to know that you were standing by your values and choosing not to allow people to cross your boundaries like this?

_____

_____

_____

_____

_____

_____

_____

_____

_____

_____

_____

_____

Imagine a scenario where observing your thoughts without judgment could bring you clarity.

How would this awareness change your perspective on the situation? For example, imagine that you're in the middle of a meeting and you are about to present something to the rest of the room. You are stressed and worried—public speaking *isn't* your forte. You have two options: to give into the stress, or to focus on the present moment. What do you prefer doing? Do you think you can observe your thoughts and rationalize the situation? Can you focus on the present moment, instead of thinking about all the "what ifs"?

_____

_____

_____

_____

_____

_____

_____

_____

_____

_____

Think about a time when mixing your intentions and actions created balance.

For example, think about a time when you decided to act intentionally – doing something purposely, thinking deeply about yourself, about what the best option was, and so on. Do you feel like the outcome was a better balance? How can you apply this to the rest of your life?

_____

_____

_____

_____

_____

_____

_____

_____

_____

_____

_____

_____

_____

Think about a moment where focusing on your breath (which is an important part of mindfulness) gave you peace in a tense situation.

How did this change the dynamics of the moment? Did you feel like you had more control over the situation? Did you feel like you were better equipped to deal with the situation you had on your hands? Did you feel calm, relaxed, and less overwhelmed afterwards?

_____

_____

_____

_____

_____

_____

_____

_____

_____

_____

_____

_____

_____

Have you ever used gratitude? If so, how did it feel? If not, try it today, and see how you feel at the end of the day.

Gratitude is something that can instantly make you happier. Whenever you have a bad day, take a few minutes to point out three to five things that you are grateful for. This can help you put things into perspective, and hence, can make you feel at ease.

_____

_____

_____

_____

_____

_____

_____

_____

_____

_____

_____

_____

_____

_____

Conclusion

Wow, what a journey this has been! The path to ease is one that might not have felt easy at the beginning of this workbook. And yet, by now, you are far better equipped to continue with your life and feel empowered with ease.

Life doesn't have to be hard, complicated, or overwhelming. It can be done with *ease*. You can enjoy your life and everything that it has to offer!

Throughout the process, make sure to care about yourself. Doing the inner work and healing is necessary to accomplish your end goal of achieving ease, and hence, living the life of your dreams! And I have great news for you: with this book completed, you have made huge steps towards this. In fact, some of you may be right there.

If you aren't, don't give up. Living a life of ease and healing yourself from your past and shadow self can take a long time. But with effort comes rewards. So, keep working on yourself, and you will one day enjoy the fruits of your labor.